LAND OF THE POETS

LAKE DISTRICT

Photographs by

DAVID LYONS

PRC

For Maria and other lovers of the smell of moss.

This edition first published in 1996 by the
Promotional Reprint Company Ltd,
Kiln House,
210 New Kings Road,
London SW6 4NZ.

Photographs © David Lyons 1996
Design and Layout © PRC Ltd 1996

ISBN 1 85648 325 8

Printed and bound in China

INTRODUCTION

Few spots on earth can have inspired as many lines of poetry as the Lake District in the far northwest of England. The crags and hills and lakes have been formed in a harmony of proportion, line and colour which manages to convey all the drama and grandeur of more Alpine regions with the quieter, more domestic and intimate pleasures of the best of rural England. The area has engaged a nation of poets and lovers of poetry, and provided a fertile cradling for the great inspirational presence of William Wordsworth, whose genius strides through romantic literature just like the paths stride over the Lakeland fells, leading others to discover fresh vistas.

Wordsworth took the mountain streams, summer lakeside evenings and the hoary crags and wove them with the stories of shepherds and cottagers, his Esthwaite and Grasmere neighbours. His was a retelling of tales which touched many a city dweller who, enchanted by his poetic descriptions, had their delight confirmed and multiplied when they themselves set foot on his hills. This land was real. The young Wordsworth and his friend Samuel Taylor Coleridge set out a new map of the landscape of poetry where 'Presences of Nature' were experienced first hand and their essence distilled into words. A kind of alchemy took place — like the reawakening of some pagan life force dormant in England for centuries. Since then Wordsworth's poetry at its best has given a kind of magical key to its readers and opened up for them a closer view of the landscape — so that they can see into the heart of things.

Surprisingly, until recent years, the Lake District has bred very few native poets. This anthology is drawn mainly from Wordsworth and his near contemporaries up until the first half of this century. In that time most of the writers were 'offcomers', who either came to live in the Lake District or were frequent visitors and adopted it as their second home — a place where they would choose to be if they didn't have to be somewhere else. But they all shared in common the sense of the overpowering presence which is the special landscape of this place. Today more than ever, rarely can a place have been so truly loved by so many people. From rock climbers to ramblers this land now belongs to everyone to discover and enjoy as they please.

I have lived in Langdale, the valley next door to Wordsworth's, for some 12 years now and from there my photography takes me to many lands. But when I come home I am still surprised by the sheer variety and beauty of the Lakes. And if sometimes I find the modern-day presence of the giant Wordsworth a little oppressive, I can always call down the road and spend a few hours with John Ruskin, whose crystal eyes maybe describe more clearly the world as glimpsed by a photographer; or I can walk a mile with young Hartley Coleridge, Samuel's son, who could draw a few lines with the unpretentious simplicity and directness of Robbie Burns.

I have spent many days with a camera in what is obviously a richly inspirational environment and have often felt unable to find anything worth photographing. On these days I waste a lot of film for no result. The harder I try the more difficult it becomes to see. I know the problem does not lie in the woods or the hillsides or in the mountain becks because at other times it seems almost effortless, as if I have been offered a gift. But gifts require us to be receptive, to be open to delight. Perhaps the real lesson taught by the Lake Poets is that sometimes the finest poetry comes from just taking a walk with our eyes open.

David Lyons
Langdale, January 1996

From 'The Prelude'

A dreary moor
Was crossed, a bare ridge clomb, upon whose top
Standing alone, as from a rampart's edge,
I overlooked the bed of Windermere,
  Like a vast river, stretching in the sun.
  With exultation, at my feet I saw
Lake, islands, promontories, gleaming bays,
A universe of Nature's fairest forms
Proudly revealed with instantaneous burst,
Magnificent, and beautiful and gay.

William Wordsworth
1770-1850

Mountains

Mountains are to the rest of the body of the earth, what violent muscular action is to the body of man. The muscles and tendons of its anatomy are, in the mountain, brought out with force and convulsive energy, full of expression, passion, and strength; the plains and the lower hills are the repose and the effortless motion of the frame, when its muscles lie dormant and concealed beneath the lines of its beauty, yet ruling those lines in their every undulation. This, then, is the first grand principle of the truth of the earth. The spirit of the hills is action, that of the lowlands repose; and between these there is to be found every variety of motion and of rest, from the inactive plain, sleeping like the firmament, with cities for stars, to the fiery peaks, which, with heaving bosoms and exulting limbs, with the clouds drifting like hair from their bright foreheads, lift up their Titan hands to heaven, saying, 'I live for ever!'

John Ruskin
1819-1900

In Anticipation of Leaving School

Dear native regions, I foretell,
From what I feel at this farewell,
That, wheresoe'er my steps may tend,
And whensoe'er my course shall end,
If in that hour a single tie
Survive of local sympathy,
My soul will cast the backward view,
The longing look alone on you.

Thus, while the Sun sinks down to rest
Far in the regions of the west,
Though to the vale no parting beam
Be given, not one memorial gleam,
A lingering light he fondly throws
On the dear hills where first he rose.

William Wordsworth
1770-1850

Confessions of an Opium-Eater

Let there be a cottage, standing in a valley, eighteen miles from any town ; no spacious valley, but about two miles long by three quarters of a mile in average width, – the benefit of which provision is, that all the families resident within its circuit will compose, as it were, one larger household, personally familiar to your eye, and more or less interesting to your affections. Let the mountains be real mountains, between three and four thousand feet high, and the cottage a real cottage not (as a witty author has it) 'a cottage with a double coach-house'; let it be, in fact (for I must abide by the actual scene), a white cottage, embowered with flowering shrubs, so chosen as to unfold a succession of flowers upon the walls, and clustering around the windows, through all the months of spring, summer, and autumn; beginning, in fact, with May roses, and ending jasmine. Let it, however, not be spring, nor, summer, nor autumn; but winter, in its sternest shape. This is a most important point in the science of happiness. And I am surprised to see people overlook it, and think it matter of congratulation that winter is going, or, if coming, is not likely to be a severe one. On the contrary, I put up a petition, annually, for as much snow, hail, frost, or storm of one kind or other, as skies can possibly afford us. Surely everybody is aware of the divine pleasures which attend a winter fireside, candles at four o'clock, warm hearth-rugs, tea, a fair tea-maker, shutters closed, curtains flowing in ample draperies on the floor, whilst the wind and rain are raging audibly without...

All these are items in the description of a winter evening which must surely be familiar to everybody born in a high latitude. And it is evident that most of these delicacies, like ice-cream, require a very low temperature of the atmosphere to produce them: they are fruits which cannot be ripened without weather stormy or inclement, in some way or other. I am not '*particular*,' as people say, whether it be snow, or black frost, or wind so strong that (as Mr.-- says) 'you may lean your back against it like a post.' I can put up even with rain, provided that it rains cats and dogs; but something of the sort I must have, and if I have not, I think myself in a manner ill used: for why am I called on to pay so heavily for winter, in coals, and candles, and various privations that will occur even to gentlemen, if I am not to have the article good of its kind?

Thomas de Quincey
1785-1859

Lines from 'The Prelude'

There, 'tis the shepherd's task the winter long
To wait upon the storms: of their approach
Sagacious, into sheltering coves he drives
His flock, and thither from the homestead bears
A toilsome burden up the craggy ways,
And deals it out, their regular nourishment
Strewn on the frozen snow. And when the spring
Looks out, and all the pastures dance with lambs,
And when the flock, with warmer weather,climbs
Higher and higher, him his office leads
To watch their goings, whatsoever track
The wanderers choose. For this he quits his home
At day-spring, and no sooner doth the sun
Begin to strike him with a fire-like heat,
Than he lies down upon some shining rock,
And breakfasts with his dog. When they have stolen,
As is their wont, a pittance from strict time,
For rest not needed or exchange of love,
Then from his couch he starts; and now his feet
Crush out a livelier fragrance from the flowers
Of lowly thyme, by Nature's skill enwrought
In the wild turf : the lingering dews of morn
Smoke round him, as from hill to hill he hies,
His staff protending like a hunter's spear,
Or by its aid leaping from crag to crag,
And o'er the brawling beds of unbridged streams.
Philosophy, methinks, at Fancy's call,
Might deign to follow him through what he does
Or sees in his day's march ; himself he feels,
In those vast regions where his service lies,
A freeman, wedded to his life of hope
And hazard, and hard labour interchanged
With that majestic indolence so dear
To native man. A rambling schoolboy, thus
I felt his presence in his own domain,
As of a lord and master, or a power,

Or genius, under Nature, under God,
Presiding; and severest solitude
Had more commanding looks when he was there.
When up the lonely brooks on rainy days
Angling I went, or trod the trackless hills
By mists bewildered, suddenly mine eyes
Have glanced upon him distant a few steps,
In size a giant, stalking through thick fog,
His sheep like Greenland bears; or, as he stepped
Beyond the boundary line of some hill-shadow,
His form hath flashed upon me, glorified
By the deep radiance of the setting sun:
Or him have I descried in distant sky,
A solitary object and sublime,
Above all height! like an aerial cross
Stationed alone upon a spiry rock
Of the Chartreuse, for worship. Thus was man
Ennobled outwardly before my sight,
And thus my heart was early introduced
To an unconscious love and reverence
Of human nature; hence the human form
To me became an index of delight,
Of grace and honour, power and worthiness.

William Wordsworth
1770-1850

Written on the Banks of Wastwater During a Calm

Is this the lake, the cradle of the storms,
Where silence never tames the mountain-roar,
Where poets fear their self-created forms,
Or, sunk in trance severe, their God adore?
Is this the lake for ever dark and loud,
With wave and tempest, cataract and cloud?
Wondrous, O Nature, is thy sovereign power,
That gives to horror hours of peaceful mirth;
For here might beauty build her summer bower!
Lo! where yon rainbow spans the smiling earth,
And clothed in glory, through a silent shower
The mighty Sun comes forth, a god-like birth;
While, 'neath his loving eye the gentle Lake
Lies like a sleeping child too blest to wake!

Christopher North
(pseudonym of Professor John Wilson) 1785-1854

Near Blea Tarn

We scaled, without a track to ease our steps,
A steep ascent; and reached a dreary plain,
With a tumultuous waste of huge hill-tops
Before us, savage region! which I paced
Dispirited: when, all at once, behold!
Beneath our feet, a little lowly vale,
A lowly vale, and yet uplifted high
Among the mountains. . . .
Urn-like it was in shape, deep as an urn;
With rocks encompassed, save that to the south
Was one small opening, where a heath-clad ridge
Supplied a boundary less abrupt and close;
A quiet treeless nook, with two green fields,
A liquid pool that glittered in the sun,
And one bare dwelling . . . .

Full many a spot
Of hidden beauty have I chanced to espy
Among the mountains; never one like this
So lonesome, and so perfectly secure;
Not melancholy – no, for it is green
And bright and fertile. . . .
– In rugged arms how softly does it lie.
How tenderly protected! . . . were this
Man's only dwelling, sole appointed seat,
First, last, and single in the breathing world,
It could not be more quiet: peace is here
Or nowhere.

William Wordsworth
1770-1850

Prayer on Skiddaw

I thought I should like a long, quiet day on Skiddaw by myself, so I gave Crawley some work at home, in packing stones, and took my hammer and compass, and sauntered up leisurely. It was threatening rain, in its very beauty of stillness, - no sunshine - only dead calm under grey sky. I sate down for a while on the highest shoulder of the hill under the summit - in perfect calm of air - as if in a room! Then, suddenly - in a space of not more than ten minutes - vast volumes of white cloud formed in the west. When I first sate down, all the Cumberland mountains, from Scawfell to the Penrith Hills, lay round me like a clear model, cut in wood - I never saw anything so ridiculously clear - great masses 2000 feet high looking like little green bosses under one's hand. Then as I said, in ten minutes, the white clouds formed, and came foaming from the west towards Skiddaw; then answering white fleeces started into being on Scawfell and Helvellyn - and the moment they were formed, the unnatural clearness passed away, and the mountains, where still visible, resumed their proper distances. I rose and went on along the stately ridge towards the summit, hammering and poking about for fibrous quartz. . . . It was very beautiful, with the white cloud filling all the western valley - and the air still calm - and the desolate peak and moors, motionless for many a league, but for the spots of white - which were sheep, one knew - and were sometimes to be seen to move.

I always - even in my naughtiest times - had a way of praying on hill summits, when I could get quiet on them; so I knelt on a bit of rock to pray - and there came suddenly into my mind the clause of the Litany, 'for all that travel by land or water,' etc. So I prayed it, and you can't think what a strange, intense meaning it had up there - one felt so much more the feebleness of the feeble there, where all was wild and strong, and there 'Show thy pity on all prisoners and captives' came so wonderfully where I had the feeling of absolutely boundless liberty. I could rise from kneeling and dash away to any quarter of heaven - east or west or south or north - with leagues of moorland tossed one after another like sea waves.

John Ruskin
1819-1900

A Carol of the Skiddaw Shepherds

The shepherds on the fellside
  That is by Bethany
Had not on finger
  Redder blains than we.
  Jesu, that art God's light,
  Warm us in the cold night.

The yowes that men were minding
  Long and long ago,
Were not more like to die
  Than ours in the snow.
  Jesu, that knows Thy sheep,
  Skiddaw yowes tend and keep.

The angels that were singing
  Long and long agone,
Were not a whiter host
  Than snowflakes fa'ing down.
  Jesu, the true Fold,
  Gird us on the rocks cold.

Edmund Casson

Untitled

There is a power to bless
In hillside loneliness –
In tarns and dreary places –
A virtue in the brook,
A freshness in the look
Of mountains' joyless faces –
And so, when life is dull
Or when my heart is full
Because my dreams have frowned,
I wander up the rills
To stones and tarns and hills –
I go there to be crowned.

Frederick William Faber
1814-1863

A Remembrance of Grasmere

O vale and lake, within your mountain-urn
Smiling so tranquilly, and set so deep!
Oft doth your dreamy loveliness return,
Colouring the tender shadows of my sleep
With light Elysian; for the hues that steep
Your shores in melting lustre, seem to float
On golden clouds from spirit-lands remote,
Isles of the blest; and in our memory keep
Their place with holiest harmonies. Fair scene,
Most loved by evening and her dewy star!
Oh! ne'er may man, with touch unhallowed jar
The perfect music of thy charm serene!
Still, still unchanged, may one sweet region wear
Smiles that subdue the soul to love, and tears, and prayer.

Felicia Dorothea Hemans
1793-1835

From 'The Prelude'

Oh, there is blessing in this gentle breeze
A vis'tant that while it fans my cheek
Doth seem half-conscious of the joy it brings
From the green fields, and from yon azure sky
Whate'er its mission, the soft breeze can come
To none more grateful than to me escaped
From the vast city. . . .
        . . . . In what vale
Shall be my harbour? underneath what grove
Shall I take up my home? and what clear stream
Shall with its murmur lull me into rest?
The earth is all before me. With a heart
Joyous, nor scared at its own liberty,
I look about; and should the chosen guide
Be nothing better than a wandering cloud,
I cannot miss my way . . . .
        . . . . Whither shall I turn
By road or pathway, or through trackless field,
Up hill or down, or shall some floating thing
Upon the river point me out my course?

William Wordsworth
1770-1850

There Was a Boy

There was a boy; ye knew him well ye cliffs
And islands of Winander! – many a time,
At evening, when the earliest stars began
To move along the edges of the hills,
Rising or setting, would he stand alone,
Beneath the trees, or by the glimmering lake;
And there, with fingers interwoven, both hands
Pressed closely palm to palm and to his mouth
Uplifted, he, as through an instrument,
Blew mimic hootings to the silent owls,
That they might answer him. – And they would shout
Across the watery vale, and shout again,
Responsive to his call, – with quivering peals,
And long halloos, and screams, and echoes loud
Redoubled and redoubled; concourse wild
Of jocund din! And, when there came a pause
Of silence such as baffled his best skill:
Then, sometimes, in that silence while he hung
Listening, a gentle shock of mild surprise
Has carried far into his heart the voice
Of mountain torrents; or the visible scene
Would enter unawares into his mind
With all its solemn imagery, its rocks,
Its woods, and that uncertain heaven received
Into the bosom of the steady lake.

William Wordsworth
1770-1850

Lines from 'The Excursion'

'Oh! what a joy it were, in vigorous health,
To have a body (this our vital frame
With shrinking sensibility endued,
And all the nice regards of flesh and blood)
And to the elements surrender it
As if it were a spirit! – How divine
The liberty, for frail, for mortal man
To roam at large among unpeopled glens
And mountainous retirements, only trod
By devious footsteps; regions consecrate
To oldest time! and, reckless of the storm
That keeps the raven quiet in her nest,
Be as a presence or a motion – one
Among the many there; and while the mists
Flying, and rainy vapours, call out shapes
And phantoms from the crags and solid earth
As fast as a musician scatters sounds
Out of an instrument; and while the streams
(As at a first creation and in haste
To exercise their untried faculties)

Descending from the region of the clouds,
And starting from the hollows of the earth
More multitudinous every moment, rend
Their way before them – what a joy to roam
An equal among mightiest energies;
And haply sometimes with articulate voice,
Amid the defending tumult, scarcely heard
By him that utters it, exclaim aloud,
"Rage on, ye elements! let moon and stars
Their aspects lend, and mingle in their turn
With this commotion (ruinous though it be)
From day to night, from night to day, prolonged!" '

William Wordsworth
1770-1850

The Hills

Now men there be that love the plain
  With yellow cornland dressed,
And others love the sleepy vales
  Where lazy cattle rest;
But some men love the ancient hills,
  And these have chosen best.

For in the hills a man may go
  For ever as he list
And see a net of distant worlds
  Where streams and valleys twist
A league below, and seem to hold
  The whole earth in his fist.

Or if he treads the dales beneath
  A new delight is his,
For every crest's a kingdom-edge
  Whose conqueror he is,
And every fell the frontier
  Of unguessed emperies.

And when the clouds are on the land
  In shelter he may lie,
And watch adown the misty glens
  The rain go marching by,
Along the silent flank of fells
  Whose heads are in the sky.

And in the hills are crystal tarns
  As deep as maidens' eyes,
About whose edge at middle-noon
  The heavy sunshine lies,
And deep therein the troll-folk dwell
  Can make men wondrous wise.

The gorse of spring is like a host
  Of warriors in gold,
And summer heather like a cloak
  Of purple on the wold,
While autumn's russet bracken is
  Monks' livery of old.

Our lord the sun knows every land,
  But most he loves the fells;
At morning break his earliest torch
  Upon their summit dwells,
At eve he lingers there to catch
  The sound of vesper bells.

The men who dwell among the hills
  Have eyes both strong and kind,
For as they go about their works
  In Heaven's sun and wind,
The spirit of the 'stablished hills
  Gives them the steadfast mind.

William Noel Hodgson
1893-1916

Canny Cummerlan

Yer buik-larn'd wise gentry that's seen monie counties,
  May preach and palaver, and brag as they will
O' mountains, lakes, valleys, woods, watters, and meadows,
  But canny auld Cummerlan caps them aw still:
It's true, we've nae palaces sheynin amang us,
  Nor marble tall towers to catch the weak eye;
But we've monie feyne cassels, where fit our brave fadders,
  When Cummerland cud onie county defy.

Whea that hes climb'd Skiddaw, has seen sec a prospec,
  Where fells frown owre fells, and in majesty vie?
Whea that hes seen Keswick, can count hawf its beauties,
  May e'en try to count hawf the stars i' the sky:
Theer's Ullswater, Bassenthwaite, Wastwater, Derwent,
  That thousands on thousands ha'e travell'd to view;
The langer they gaze, still the mair they may wonder,
  And ay, as they wonder, may fin summet new.

Robert Anderson
Published c1820

Home at Grasmere

Embrace me then, ye Hills, and close me in;
Now in the clear and open day I feel
Your guardianship; I take it to my heart;'
Tis like the solemn shelter of the night.
But I would call thee beautiful, for mild,
And soft, and gay, and beautiful thou art
Dear Valley, having in thy face a smile
Though peaceful, full of gladness. Thou art pleased,
Pleased with thy crags and woody steeps, thy Lake,
Its one green island and its winding shores;
The multitude of little rocky hills,
Thy Church and cottages of mountain stone
Clustered like stars some few, but single most,
And lurking dimly in their shy retreats,
Or glancing at each other cheerful looks
Like separated stars with clouds between.
What want we? have we not perpetual streams
Warm woods, and sunny hills, and fresh green fields,
And mountains not less green, and flocks and herds,
And thickets full of songsters, and the voice
Of lordly birds, an unexpected sound
Heard now and then from morn to latest eve,

Admonishing the man who walks below
Of solitude and silence in the sky?
These have we, and a thousand nooks of earth
Have also these, but nowhere else is found,
Nowhere (or is it fancy?) can be found
The one sensation that is here; 'tis here,
Here as it found its way into my heart
In childhood, here as it abides by day,
By night, here only; or in chosen minds
That take it with them hence, wher'er they go.
- Tis, (but I cannot name it) 'tis the sense
Of majesty, and beauty, and repose,
A blended holiness of earth and sky
Something that makes this individual spot,
This small abiding-place of many men,
A termination, and a last retreat,
A centre, come from wheresoe'er you will,
A Whole without dependence or defect,
Made for itself, and happy in itself,
Perfect Contentment, Unity entire.

William Wordsworth
1770-1850

Outward Bound

There's a waterfall I'm leaving
  Running down the rocks in foam,
There's a pool for which I'm grieving
  Near the water-ouzel's home;
And it's there that I'd be lying,
  With the heather close at hand,
And the curlews faintly crying
  'Mid the wastes of Cumberland.

While the midnight watch is winging
  Thoughts of other days arise,
I can hear the river singing
  Like the saints in Paradise;
I can see the water winking
  Like the merry eyes of Pan,
And the slow half-pounder sinking
  By the bridge's granite span.

Ah! to win them back and clamber
  Braced anew with winds I love,
From the river's stainless amber
  To the morning mist above,
See through cloud-rifts rent asunder,
  Like a painted scroll unfurled,
Ridge and hollow rolling under
  To the fringes of the world.

Now the weary guard are sleeping,
  Now the great propellers churn,
Now the harbour lights are creeping
  Into emptiness astern,
While the sentry wakes and watches
  Plunging triangles of light
Where the water leaps and catches
  At our escort in the night.

Great their happiness who, seeing
  Still with unbenighted eyes
Kin of theirs who gave them being,
  Sun and earth that made them wise,
Die and feel their embers quicken
  Year by year in summer time
When the cotton grasses thicken
  On the hills they used to climb.

Shall we also be as they be,
  Mingled with our mother clay,
Or return no more it may be?
  Who has knowledge, who shall say?
Yet we hope that from the bosom
  Of our shaggy father Pan,

When the earth breaks into blossom
  Richer from the dust of man,

Though the high gods smite and slay us,
  Though we come not whence we go,
As the host of Menelaus
  Came there many years ago;
Yet the self-same wind shall bear us
  From the same departing place
Out across the Gulf of Saros
  And the Peaks of Samothrace:

We shall pass in summer weather
  We shall come at eventide,
Where the fells stand up together
  And all quiet things abide;
Mixed with cloud and wind and river
  Sun distilled in dew and rain,
One with Cumberland for ever,
  We shall not go forth again.

Noel Oxland
1895-1915

Lines from 'Influence of Natural Objects'

And in the frosty season, when the sun
Was set, and, visible for many a mile,
The cottage-windows through the twilight blazed,
I heeded not the summons : happy time
It was indeed for all of us; for me
It was a time of rapture! Clear and loud
The village-clock tolled six - I wheeled about,
Proud and exulting like an untired horse
That cares not for his home. - All shod with steel
We hissed along the polished ice, in games
Confederate, imitative of the chase
And woodland pleasures, - the resounding horn,
The pack loud-chiming, and the hunted hare.
So through the darkness and the cold we flew,
And not a voice was idle: with the din
Smitten, the precipices rang aloud;
The leafless trees and every icy crag
Tinkled like iron; while far-distant hills
Into the tumult sent an alien sound
Of melancholy, not unnoticed, while the stars,
Eastward, were sparkling clear, and in the west

The orange sky of evening died away.
Not seldom from the uproar I retired
Into a silent bay, or sportively
Glanced sideway, leaving the tumultuous throng,
To cut across the reflex of a star;
Image, that, flying still before me, gleamed
Upon the glassy plain: and oftentimes,
When we had given our bodies to the wind,
And all the shadowy banks on either side
Came sweeping through the darkness, spinning still
The rapid line of motion, then at once
Have I, reclining back upon my heels,
Stopped short; yet still the solitary cliffs
Wheeled by me - even as if the earth had rolled
With visible motion her diurnal round !
Behind me did they stretch in solemn train,
Feebler and feebler, and I stood and watched
Till all was tranquil as a summer sea.

William Wordsworth
1770-1850

Lines from 'The Prelude'

Ye motions of delight that haunt the sides
Of the green hills; ye breezes and soft airs,
Whose subtle intercourse with breathing flowers,
Feelingly watched, might teach Man's haughty race
How without injury to take, to give
Without offence; ye who, as if to show
The wondrous influence of power gently used,
Bend the complying heads of lordly pines,
And, with a touch, shift the stupendous clouds
Through the whole compass of the sky; ye brooks,
Muttering along the stones, a busy noise
By day, a quiet sound in silent night;
Ye waves, that out of the great deep steal forth
In a calm hour to kiss the pebbly shore,
Not mute, and then retire, fearing no storm;
And you, ye groves, whose ministry it is
To interpose the covert of your shades,
Even as a sleep, between the heart of man
And outward troubles. . . .
Oh! that I had a music and a voice
Harmonious as your own, that I might tell
What ye have done for me.

William Wordsworth
1770-1850

Helvellyn

I climbed the dark brow of the mighty Helvellyn,
  Lakes and mountains beneath me gleamed misty and wide;
All was still - save by fits, when the eagle was yelling,
  And, starting around me, the echoes replied.
On the right, Striding Edge round the Red Tarn was bending,
And Catchedecam its left verge was defending,
One huge nameless rock in front was impending,
  When I marked the sad spot where the wanderer died.

Dark green was that spot, 'mid the brown mountain heather,
  Where the pilgrim of nature lay stretched in decay,
Like the corpse of an outcast, abandoned to weather,
  Till the mountain winds wasted the tenantless clay:
Not yet quite deserted, though lonely extended,
For faithful in death, his mute favourite attended,
The much-loved remains of his master defended,
  And chased the hill-fox and the raven away.

How long did'st thou think that his silence was slumber –
  When the wind waved his garments how oft did'st thou start –
How many long days and long nights did'st thou number,
  Ere he faded before thee, the friend of thy heart?
And, ah! was it meet that no requiem read o'er him;
No mother to weep, and no friend to deplore him;
And thou, little guardian, alone stretched before him,
  Unhonoured the pilgrim from life should depart?

When a prince to the fate of a peasant has yielded,
  The tapestry waves dark round the dim-lighted hall;
With escutcheons of silver the coffin is shielded,
  And the pages stand mute by the canopied pall;
Through the courts, at deep midnight, the torches are gleaming,
In the proudly arched chapel the banners are beaming,
Far adown the long aisle sacred music is streaming,
  Lamenting a chief of the people should fall.

But meeter for thee, gentle lover of nature,
  To lay down thy head like the meek mountain lamb,
When, wildered, he drops from some rock high in stature,
  And draws his last breath by the side of his dam:
And more stately thy couch by this desert lake lying,
Thy obsequies sung by the gray plover flying,
With but one faithful friend to witness thy dying,
  In the arms of Helvellyn and Catchedecam.

Walter Scott
1771-1832

The Langdale Pikes

To steep and difficult descent
Trusting ourselves, we wound from crag to crag
Where passage could be won.

I could not, ever and anon, forbear
To glance an upward look on two huge Peaks,
That from some other vale peered into this.
...Many are the notes
Which, in his tuneful course, the wind draws forth
From rocks, woods, caverns, heaths, and dashing shores;
And well those lofty brethren bear their part
In the wild concert – chiefly when the storm
Rides high; then all the upper air they fill
With roaring sound, that ceases not to flow
Like smoke, along the level of the blast,
In mighty current; theirs too is the song
Of steam and headlong flood that seldom fails;
And, in the grim and breathless hour of noon,
Methinks that I have heard them echo back

The thunder's greeting. Nor have nature's laws
Left them ungifted with a power to yield
Music of finer tone; a harmony,
So do I call it, though it be the hand
Of silence, though there be no voice; – the clouds,
The mist, the shadows, light of golden suns,
Motions of moonlight, all come thither, – touch
And have an answer – thither come and shape
A language not unwelcome to sick hearts
And idle spirits: there the sun himself
Rests his substantial orb; between those heights
And on the top of either pinnacle,
More keenly than elsewhere in night's blue vault,
Sparkle the stars, as of their station proud.

William Wordsworth
1770-1850

September

The dark green Summer, with its massive hues,
Fades into Autumn's tincture manifold.
A gorgeous garniture of fire and gold
The high slope of the ferny hill indues.
The mists of morn in slumbering layers diffuse
O'er glimmering rock, smooth lake, and spiked array
Of hedge-row thorns a unity of grey.
All things appear their tangible form to lose
In ghostly vastness. But anon the gloom
Melts, as the Sun puts off his muddy veil;
And now the birds their twittering songs resume,
All Summer silent in the leafy dale.
In Spring they piped of love on every tree,
But now they sing the song of memory.

Hartley Coleridge
1796-1849

To Echo

Where Keswick's cliffs o'erhang the dale,
Responsive to the Shepherd's tale,
Oft 'midst its wild romantic grots,
I hear thy long-protracted notes.
O may no clarions rude invade
Its peaceful vale, its sylvan shade;
But, with the rural choir around,
May thy soft symphonies be found;
And when I hear the Shepherd's song,
The bleating flocks that range along,
 The breeze that, through the silent grove,
 Bears the soft sigh that steals from love;
 The Woodman's oft-repeated stroke,
 The stream that falls from hanging rock,
 The dashing of the neighb'ring mill,
 When all around is dark and still;
 The sweeping oars that gently break
 The slumbers of the peaceful lake,
 The music of the vocal lawn,
 The Hunter's horn at Morning's-dawn
 O! when I hear their chorus swell,
 Sweet Echo! give it to thy shell.

Thomas Sanderson
Published c1800

Ode to Tranquillity

Tranquillity! thou better name
Than all the family of Fame!
Thou ne'er wilt my riper age
To low intrigue, or factious rage;
For oh! dear child of thoughtful Truth,
To thee I gave my early youth,
And left the bark, and blest the steadfast shore,
Ere yet the tempest rose and scared me with its roar.

Who late and lingering seeks thy shrine,
On him but seldom, Power divine,
Thy spirit rests! Satiety
And Sloth, poor counterfeits of thee,
Mock the tired worldling. Idle Hope
And dire Remembrance interlope,
To vex the feverish slumber of the mind:
The bubble floats before, the spectre stalks behind.

But me thy gentle hand will lead
At morning through the accustomed mead;
And in the sultry summer's heat
Will build me up a mossy seat;
And when the gust of Autumn crowds,
And breaks the busy moonlight clouds,
Thou best the thought canst raise, the heart attune,
Light as the busy clouds, calm as the gliding moon.

The feeling heart, the searching soul,
To thee I dedicate the whole!
And while within myself I trace
The greatness of some future race,
Aloof with hermit-eye I scan
The present works of present man –
A wild and dream-like trade of blood and guile,
Too foolish for a tear, too wicked for a smile!

Samuel Taylor Coleridge
1772-1834

Frost at Midnight

The frost performs its secret ministry,
Unhelped by any wind. The owlet's cry
Came loud – and hark, again! loud as before.
The inmates of my cottage, all at rest,
Have left me to that solitude, which suits
Abstruser musings: save that at my side
My cradled infant slumbers peacefully.
'Tis calm indeed! so calm, that it disturbs
And vexes meditation with its strange
And extreme silentness. Sea, hill, and wood,
This populous village! Sea, and hill, and wood,
With all the numberless goings on of life,
Inaudible as dreams! the thin blue flame
Lies on my low burnt fire, and quivers not;
Only that film, which fluttered on the grate,
Still flutters there, the sole unquiet thing.
Methinks, its motion in this hush of nature
Gives it dim sympathies with me who live,
Making it a companionable form,
Whose puny flaps and freaks the idling Spirit
By its own moods interprets, every where
Echo or mirror seeking of itself,
And makes a toy of Thought.

          But O! how oft,
How oft, at school, with most believing mind,
Presageful, have I gazed upon the bars,
To watch that fluttering stranger! and as oft
With unclosed lids, already had I dreamt
Of my sweet birth-place, and the old church-tower,
Whose bells, the poor man's only music, rang
From morn to evening, all the hot Fair-day,
So sweetly, that they stirred and haunted me
With a wild pleasure, falling on mine ear
Most like articulate sounds of things to come!
So gazed I, till the soothing things I dreamt
Lulled me to sleep, and sleep prolonged my dreams!
And so I brooded all the following morn,
Awed by the stern preceptor's face, mine eye
Fixed with mock study on my swimming book:
Save if the door half opened, and I snatched
A hasty glance, and still my heart leaped up,
For still I hoped to see the stranger's face,
Townsman, or aunt, or sister more beloved,
My play-mate when we both were clothed alike!

          Dear Babe, that sleepest cradled by my side,
Whose gentle breathings, heard in this deep calm,
Fill up the interspersed vacancies
And momentary pauses of the thought!
My babe so beautiful! it thrills my heart
With tender gladness, thus to look at thee,

And think that thou shalt learn far other lore
And in far other scenes! For I was reared
In the great city, pent 'mid cloisters dim,
And saw nought lovely but the sky and stars.
But thou, my babe! shalt wander like a breeze
By lakes and sandy shores, beneath the crags
Of ancient mountain, and beneath the clouds,
Which image in their bulk both lakes and shores
And mountain crags: so shalt thou see and hear
The lovely shapes and sound intelligible
Of that eternal language, which thy God
Utters, who from eternity doth teach
Himself in all, and all things in himself.
Great universal Teacher! he shall mould
Thy spirit, and by giving make it ask.

          Therefore all seasons shall be sweet to thee,
Whether the summer clothe the general earth
With greenness, or the redbreast sit and sing
Betwixt the tufts of snow on the bare branch
Of mossy apple-tree, while the nigh thatch
Smokes in the sun-thaw; whether the eve-drops fall
Heard only in the trances of the blast,
Or if the secret ministry of frost
Shall hang them up in silent icicles,
Quietly shining to the quiet Moon.

Samuel Taylor Coleridge
1772-1834

Lines from 'The River Duddon'

A dark plume fetch me from yon blasted yew,
Perched on whose top the Danish Raven croaks;
Aloft, the imperial Bird of Rome invokes
Departed ages, shedding where he flew
Loose fragments of wild wailing, that bestrew
The clouds and thrill the chambers of the rocks;
And into silence hush the timorous flocks,
That calmly couching while the nightly dew
Moistened each fleece, beneath the twinkling stars
Slept amid that lone Camp on Hardknot's height,
Whose Guardians bent the knee to Jove and Mars.

William Wordsworth
1770-1850

Lines from 'Michael'

The mountains have all open'd out themselves,
And made a hidden valley of their own.
No habitation there is seen; but such
As journey thither find themselves alone
With a few sheep, with rocks and stones, and kites
That overhead are sailing in the sky.

And grossly that man errs, who should suppose
That the green valleys, and the streams and rocks,
Were things indifferent to the shepherds thoughts.
Fields, where with cheerful spirits he had breathed
The common air; the hills, which he so oft
Had climb'd with vigorous steps;
 which had impress'd
So many incidents upon his mind
Of hardship, skill, or courage, joy, or fear;
Which like a book preserved the memory
Of the dumb animals, whom he had saved,
Had fed or shelter'd, linking to such acts,
So grateful in themselves, the certainty
Of honourable gain; these fields, these hills,
Which were his living being, even more
Than his own blood – what could they less? had laid
Strong hold on his affections, were to him
A pleasurable feeling of blind love,
The pleasure which there is in life itself.

William Wordsworth
1770-1850

Lines from 'The Excursion'

Already had the sun,
Sinking with less than ordinary state,
Attained his western bound; but rays of light –
Now suddenly diverging from the orb
Retired behind the mountain tops or veiled
By the dense air – shot upwards to the crown
Of the blue firmament – aloft, and wide:
And multitudes of little floating clouds,
Through their ethereal texture pierced – ere we,
Who saw, of change were conscious – had become
Vivid as fire; clouds separately poised, –
Innumerable multitude of forms
Scattered through half the circle of the sky;
And giving back, and shedding each on each,
With prodigal communion, the bright hues
Which from the unapparent fount of glory
They had imbibed, and ceased not to receive.
That which the heavens displayed, the liquid deep
Repeated; but with unity sublime!

William Wordsworth
1770-1850

Lines from 'An Evening Walk'

How pleasant, as the sun declines, to view
The spacious landscape change in form and hue!
Here, vanish, as in mist, before a flood
Of bright obscurity, hill, lawn, and wood;
There, objects, by the searching beams betrayed,
Come forth, and here retire in purple shade;
Even the white stems of birch, the cottage white,
Soften their glare before the mellow light.

William Wordsworth
1770-1850

35

My Days Among the Dead are Past

My days among the Dead are past;
Around me I behold,
Where'er these casual eyes are cast,
The mighty minds of old;
My never-failing friends are they,
With whom I converse day by day.

With them I take delight in weal,
And seek relief in woe;
And while I understand and feel
How much to them I owe,
My cheeks have often been bedew'd
With tears of thoughtful gratitude.

My thoughts are with the Dead, with them
I live in long-past years,
Their virtues love, their faults condemn,
Partake their hopes and fears,
And from their lessons seek and find
Instruction with an humble mind.

My hopes are with the Dead, anon
My place with them be,
And I with them shall travel on
Through all Futurity;
Yet leaving here a name, I trust,
That will not perish in the dust.

Robert Southey
1774-1843

The Tables Turned

Up! up! my Friend, and quit your book;
Or surely you'll grow double:
Up! up! my Friend, and clear your looks;
Why all this toil and trouble?

The sun, above the mountain's head,
A freshening lustre mellow
Through all the long green fields has spread,
His first sweet evening yellow.

Books! 't is a dull and endless strife:
Come, hear the woodland linnet,
How sweet his music! on my life,
There's more of wisdom in it.

And hark ! how blithe the throstle sings!
He, too, is no mean preacher:
Come forth into the light of things,
Let Nature be your teacher.

She has a world of ready wealth,
Our minds and hearts to bless –
Spontaneous wisdom breathed by health,
Truth breathed by cheerfulness.

One impulse from a vernal wood
May teach you more of man,
Of moral evil and of good,
Than all the sages can.

Sweet is the lore which Nature brings;
Our meddling intellect
Mis-shapes the beauteous forms of things: –
We murder to dissect.

Enough of Science and of Art;
Close up those barren leaves;
Come forth, and bring with you a heart
That watches and receives.

William Wordsworth
1770-1850

The World is Too Much With Us: Late and Soon

The world is too much with us; late and soon,
Getting and spending, we lay waste our powers:
Little we see in Nature that is ours;
We have given our hearts away, a sordid boon!
This Sea that bears her bosom to the moon;
The winds that will be howling at all hours,
And are up-gathered now like sleeping flowers;
For this, for everything, we are out of tune;
It moves us not. – Great God! I'd rather be
A Pagan suckled in a creed outworn;
So might I, standing on this pleasant lea,
Have glimpses that would make me less forlorn;
Have sight of Proteus rising from the sea;
Or hear old Triton blow his wreathèd horn.

William Wordsworth
1770-1850

Ode. Intimations of Immortality

There was a time when meadow, grove, and stream,
The earth, and every common sight,
    To me did seem
    Apparelled in celestial light,
The glory and the freshness of a dream.
It is not now as it hath been of yore; –
    Turn wheresoe'er I may,
    By night or day,
The things which I have seen I now can see no more.

    The Rainbow comes and goes,
    And lovely is the Rose,
    The Moon doth with delight
Look round her when the heavens are bare,
    Waters on a starry night
    Are beautiful and fair;
    The sunshine is a glorious birth;
    But yet I know, where'er I go,
That there hath passed away a glory from the earth.

Now, while the birds thus sing a joyous song,
    And while the young lambs bound
    As to the tabor's sound,
To me alone there came a thought of grief:
A timely utterance gave that thought relief,
    And I again am strong:
The cataracts blow their trumpets from the steep;
No more shall grief of mine the season wrong;
I hear the Echoes through the mountains throng,
The Winds come to me from the fields of sleep,
    And all the earth is gay;
    Land and sea
    Give themselves up to jollity,
    And with the heart of May
    Doth every Beast keep holiday; –
    Thou Child of Joy,
Shout round me, let me hear thy shouts, thou happy
    Shepherd-boy!

Ye blessèd Creatures, I have heard the call
    Ye to each other make; I see

The heavens laugh with you in your jubilee;
    My heart is at your festival,
    My head hath its coronal,
The fulness of your bliss, I feel – I feel it all.
    Oh, evil day! if I were sullen
    While earth herself is adorning,
    This sweet May morning,
    And the children are culling
    On every side,
    In a thousand valleys far and wide,
    Fresh flowers; while the sun shines warm,
And the Babe leaps up on his Mother's arm: –
    I hear, I hear, with joy I hear!
    – But there's a Tree, of many, one,
A single Field which I have looked upon,
Both of them speak of something that is gone:
    The pansy at my feet
    Doth the same tale repeat:
Whither is fled the visionary gleam?
Where is it now, the glory and the dream?

Our birth is but a sleep and a forgetting:
The Soul that rises with us, our life's Star,
    Hath had elsewhere its setting,
    And cometh from afar;
    Not in entire forgetfulness,
    And not in utter nakedness,
But trailing clouds of glory do we come
    From God, who is our home:
Heaven lies about us in our infancy!
Shades of the prison-house begin to close
    Upon the growing Boy,
But He beholds the light, and whence it flows,
    He sees it in his joy;
The Youth, who daily farther from the east
    Must travel, still is Nature's Priest,
    And by the vision splendid
    Is on his way attended;
At length the Man perceives it die away,
And fade into the light of common day.

Earth fills her lap with pleasures of her own;
Yearnings she hath in her own natural kind,
And even with something of a Mother's mind,
    And no unworthy aim,
    The homely Nurse doth all she can
To make her Foster-child, her Inmate Man,
    Forget the glories he hath known,
And that imperial palace whence he came.

Behold the Child among the new-born blisses,
A six years' Darling of a pigmy size!
See, where 'mid work of his own hand he lies,
Fretted by sallies of his mother's kisses,
With light upon him from his father's eyes!
See, at his feet, some little plan or chart,
Some fragment from his dream of human life,
Shaped by himself with newly-learned art;
    A wedding or a festival,
    A mourning or a funeral;
      And this hath now his heart,
    And unto this he frames his song:
      Then will he fit his tongue
To dialogues of business, love, or strife;
    But it will not be long
    Ere this be thrown aside,
    And with new joy and pride
The little Actor cons another part;
Filling from time to time his 'humorous stage'
With all the Persons, down to palsied Age,
That Life brings with her in her equipage;
    As if his whole vocation
    Were endless imitation.

Thou, whose exterior semblance doth belie
    Thy Soul's immensity;
Thou best Philosopher, who yet dost keep
Thy heritage, thou Eye among the blind,
That, deaf and silent, read'st the eternal deep,
Haunted for ever by the eternal mind, –
    Mighty Prophet! Seer blest!
    On whom those truths do rest,
Which we are toiling all our lives to find,
In darkness lost, the darkness of the grave;
Thou, over whom thy Immortality
Broods like the Day, a Master o'er a Slave,
A Presence which is not to be put by;
Thou, little Child, yet glorious in the might
Of heaven-born freedom on thy being's height,
Why with such earnest pains dost thou provoke
The years to bring the inevitable yoke,
Thus blindly with thy blessedness at strife?
Full soon thy Soul shall have her earthly freight,
And custom lie upon thee with a weight,
Heavy as frost, and deep almost as life!

    O joy! that in our embers
    Is something that doth live,
    That Nature yet remembers
    What was so fugitive!
The thought of our past years in me doth breed
Perpetual benediction: not indeed
For that which is most worthy to be blest –
Delight and liberty, the simple creed
Of Childhood, whether busy or at rest,
With new-fledged hope still fluttering in his breast: –
    Not for these I raise
    The song of thanks and praise;
    But for those obstinate questionings

Of sense and outward things,
    Fallings from us, vanishings;
    Blank misgivings of a Creature
Moving about in worlds not realised,
High instincts before which our mortal Nature
Did tremble like a guilty Thing surprised:
    But for those first affections,
    Those shadowy recollections,
    Which, be they what they may,
Are yet the fountain light of all our day,
Are yet a master light of all our seeing;
    Uphold us, cherish, and have power to make
Our noisy years seem moments in the being
Of the eternal Silence: truths that wake,
    To perish never;
Which neither listlessness, nor mad endeavour,
    Nor Man nor Boy,
Nor all that is at enmity with joy,
Can utterly abolish or destroy!
    Hence in a season of calm weather,
    Though inland far we be,
Our Souls have sight of that immortal sea
    Which brought us hither,
    Can in a moment travel thither,
And see the Children sport upon the shore,
And hear the mighty waters rolling evermore.

Then sing, ye Birds, sing, sing a joyous song!
    And let the young Lambs bound
    As to the tabor's sound!
We in thought will join your throng,
    Ye that pipe and ye that play,
    Ye that through your hearts to-day
    Feel the gladness of the May!
What though the radiance which was once so bright
Be now for ever taken from my sight,
    Though nothing can bring back the hour
Of splendour in the grass, of glory in the flower;
    We will grieve not, rather find
    Strength in what remains behind;
    In the primal sympathy
    Which having been must ever be;
    In the soothing thoughts that spring
    Out of human suffering;
    In the faith that looks through death,
In years that bring the philosophic mind.

And, O ye Fountains, Meadows, Hills and Groves,
Forbode not any severing of our loves!
Yet in my heart of hearts I feel your might;
I only have relinquished one delight
To live beneath your more habitual sway.
I love the Brooks which down their channels fret,
Even more than when I tripped lightly as
they;
The innocent brightness of a new-born Day
    Is lovely yet;
The Clouds that gather round the setting sun
Do take a sober colouring from an eye
That hath kept watch o'er man's mortality;
Another race hath been, and other palms are won.
Thanks to the human heart by which we live,
Thanks to its tenderness, its joys, and fears,
To me the meanest flower that blows can give
Thoughts that do often lie too deep for tears.

William Wordsworth
1770-1850

Long Time a Child

Long time a child, and still a child, when years
Had painted manhood on my cheek, was I;
For yet I lived like one not born to die;
A thriftless prodigal of smiles and tears,
No hope I needed, and I knew no fears.
But sleep, though sweet, is only sleep, and waking,
I waked to sleep no more, at once o'ertaking
The vanguard of my age, with all arrears
Of duty on my back. Nor child, nor man,
Nor youth, nor sage, I find my head is grey,
For I have lost the race I never ran:
A rathe December blights my lagging May;
And still I am a child, tho' I be old,
Time is my debtor for my years untold.

Hartley Coleridge
1796-1849

From 'An Evening Walk'

...Quiet led me up the huddling rill,
Bright'ning with water-breaks the sombrous gill;
To where, while thick above the branches close,
In dark-brown bason its wild waves repose,
Inverted shrubs, and moss of darkest green,
Cling from the rocks, with pale wood-weeds between;
Save that, atop, the subtle sunbeams shine,
On wither'd briars that o'er the crags recline;
Sole light admitted here, a small cascade,
Illumes with sparkling foam the twilight shade.
Beyond, along the vista of the brook,
Where antique roots its bustling path o'erlook,
The eye reposes on a secret bridge
Half grey, half shagg'd with ivy to its ridge.

William Wordsworth
1770-1850

Youth and Age

Verse, a breeze mid blossoms straying,
Where Hope clung feeding, like a bee –
Both were mine! Life went a maying
With Nature, Hope, and Poesy,
When I was young!

When I was young? Ah, woeful When!
Ah! for the change 'twixt Now and Then!
This breaking house not built with hands,
This body that does me grievous wrong,
O'er aery cliffs and glittering sands,
How lightly then if flashed along: –
Like those trim skiffs, unknown of yore,
On winding lakes and rivers wide,
That ask no aid of sail or oar,
That fear no spite of wind or tide!
Nought cared this body for wind or weather
When Youth and I lived in't together.

Flowers are lovely; Love is flower-like;
Friendship is a sheltering tree;
O! the joys, that came down shower-like,
Of Friendship, Love, and Liberty,
Ere I was old!

Ere I was old? Ah woeful Ere,
Which tells me, Youth's no longer here!
O Youth! for years so many and sweet,
'Tis known, that Thou and I were one,
I'll think it but a fond conceit
It cannot be that Thou art gone!

Thy vesper-bell hath not yet toll'd:
And thou wert aye a masker bold!
What strange disguise hast now put on,
To make believe, that thou art gone?
I see these locks in silvery slips,
This drooping gait, this altered size:
But Spring-tide blossoms on thy lips,
And tears take sunshine from thine eyes!
Life is but thought: so think I will
That Youth and I are house-mates still.

Dew-drops are the gems of morning,
But the tears of mournful eve!
Where no hope is, life's a warning
That only serves to make us grieve
When we are old:

That only serves to make us grieve
With oft and tedious taking-leave,
Like some poor nigh-related guest,
That may not rudely be dismist;
Yet hath outstay'd his welcome while,
And tells the jest without the smile.

Samuel Taylor Coleridge
1772-1834

Slaty Crystallines

'It is to be remembered that these are the rocks which, on the average, will be oftenest observed, and with the greatest interest, by the human race. The central granites are too far removed, the lower rocks too common, to be carefully studied; these slaty crystallines form the noblest hills that are easily accessible, and seem to be thus calculated especially to attract observation, and reward it. Well, we begin to examine them; and first, we find a notable hardness in them, and a thorough boldness of general character, which make us regard them as very types of perfect rocks. They have nothing of the look of dried earth about them, nothing petty or limited in the display of their bulk. Where they are, they seem to form the world; no mere bank of a river here, or of a lane there, peeping out among the hedges or forests: but from the lowest valley to the highest clouds, all is theirs – one adamantine dominion and rigid authority of rock. We yield ourselves to the impression of their eternal, unconquerable stubbornness of strength, their mass seems the least yielding, least to be softened, or in anywise dealt with by external force, of all earthly substance. And, behold, as we look farther into it, it is all touched and troubled, like waves by a summer breeze; rippled, far more delicately than seas or lakes are rippled: they only undulate along their surfaces – this rock trembles through its every fibre, like the chords of an Eolian harp – like the stillest air of spring with the echoes of a child's voice. Into the heart of all those great mountains, through every tossing of their boundless crests, and deep beneath all their unfathomable defiles, flows that strange quivering of their substance. Other and weaker things seem to express their subjection to an Infinite power only by momentary terrors: as the weeds bow down before the feverish wind, and the sound of the going in the tops of the taller trees passes on before the clouds, and the fitful opening of pale spaces on the dark water, as if some invisible hand were casting dust abroad upon it, gives warning of the anger that is to come, we may well imagine that there is indeed a fear passing upon the grass, and leaves, and waters, at the presence of some great spirit commissioned to let the tempest loose; but the terror passes, and their sweet rest is perpetually restored to the pastures and the waves. Not so to the mountains. They, which at first seemed strengthened beyond the dread of any violence or change, are yet also ordained to bear upon them the symbol of a perpetual Fear: the tremor which fades from the soft lake and gliding river is sealed, to all eternity, upon the rock; and while things that pass visibly from birth to death may sometimes forget their feebleness, the mountains are made to possess a perpetual memorial of their infancy, – that infancy which the prophet saw in his vision: 'I beheld the earth, and lo, it was without form and void, and the heavens and they had no light. I beheld the mountains, and lo they *trembled*; and all the hills *moved lightly*.'

John Ruskin
1819-1900

Lines from 'Resignation'

We left, just ten years since, you say,
That wayside inn we left to-day.
Our jovial host, as forth we fare,
Shouts greeting from his easy chair.
High on a bank our leader stands,
Reviews and ranks his motley bands,
Makes clear our goal to every eye –
The valley's western boundary.
A gate swings to! our tide hath flow'd
Already from the silent road.
The valley-pastures, one by one,
Are threaded, quiet in the sun;
And now beyond the rude stone bridge
Slopes gracious up the western ridge.
Its woody border, and the last
Of its dark upland farms is past –
Cool farms, with open-lying stores,
Under their burnish'd sycamores;
All past! and through the trees we glide,
Emerging on the green hill-side.
There climbing hangs, a far-seen sign,
Our wavering, many-colour'd line;
There winds, upstreaming slowly still
Over the summit of the hill.

And now, in front, behold outspread
Those upper regions we must tread!
Mild hollows, and clear heathy swells,
The cheerful silence of the fells.
Some two hours' march with serious air,
Through the deep noontide heats we fare;
The red-grouse, springing at our sound,
Skims, now and then, the shining ground;
No life, save his and ours, intrudes
Upon these breathless solitudes.
O joy! again the farms appear.
Cool shade is there, and rustic cheer;
There springs the brook will guide us down,
Bright comrade, to the noisy town.
Lingering, we follow down; we gain
The town, the highway, and the plain.
And many a mile of dusty way,
Parch'd and road-worn, we made that day;
But, Fausta, I remember well,
That as the balmy darkness fell
We bathed our hands with speechless glee,
That night, in the wide-glimmering sea.

Matthew Arnold
1822-1888

Loughrigg Tarn

How soft these fields of pastoral beauty melt
In the clear water! neither sand nor stone
Bars herb or wild-flower from the dewy sound,
Like Spring's own voice now rippling round the Tarn.
Thou guardian Naiad of this little Lake
There oft thou liest 'mid the echoing bleat
Of lambs, that race amid the sunny gleams;
Or bee's wide murmur as it fills the broom
That yellows round thy bed.
      O gentle glades
Amid the tremulous verdure of the woods,
In steadfast smiles of more essential light,
Lying like azure streaks of placid sky
Amid the moving clouds, the Naiad loves
Your glimmering alleys, and your rustling bowers;
For there, in peace reclined, her half-closed eye
Through the long vista sees her darling Lake,
Even like herself, diffused in fair repose.
      . . . The wild vale that lies beyond,
Circled by mountains trod but by the feet
Of venturous shepherd, from all visitants,
Save the free tempests and the fowls of heaven,
Guards thee; – and wooded knolls fantastical
Seclude thy image from the gentler dale,

That by the Brathay's often-varied voice
Cheered as it winds along, in beauty fades
'Mid the green banks of joyful Windermere!
      . . . The hours
Passed tranquilly with Nature fade not away
For ever like the clouds, but in the soul
Possess a secret silent dwelling-place,
Where, with a smiling visage, memory sits.
      . . . Sweet Lake
Oft hast thou borne into my grateful heart
Thy lovely presence, with a thousand dreams
Dancing and brightening o'er thy sunny wave,
Though many a dreary mile of mist and snow
Between us interposed.

Christopher North
pseudonym of Professor John Wilson
1785-1854

Strange Fits of Passion I Have Known

Strange fits of passion I have known:
And I will dare to tell,
But in the lover's ear alone,
What once to me befell.

When she I loved was strong and gay
And like a rose in June,
I to her cottage bent my way,
Beneath the evening moon.

Upon the moon I fixed my eye,
All over the wide lea;
My horse trudged on – and we drew nigh
Those paths so dear to me.

And now we reached the orchard plot;
And, as we climbed the hill,
Towards the roof of Lucy's cot
The moon descended still.

In one of those sweet dreams I slept,
Kind Nature's gentlest boon!
And, all the while, my eyes I kept
On the descending moon.

My horse moved on; hoof after hoof
He raised, and never stopped:
When down behind the cottage roof
At once the planet dropped.

What fond and wayward thoughts will slide
Into a lover's head –
'O Mercy!' to myself I cried,
'If Lucy should be dead!'

William Wordsworth
1770-1850

Elegiac Stanzas
(suggested by a picture of Peele Castle in a storm by Sir George Beaumont)

I was thy neighbour once, thou rugged Pile!
Four summer weeks I dwelt in sight of thee:
I saw thee every day; and all the while
Thy Form was sleeping on a glassy sea.

So pure the sky, so quiet was the air!
So like, so very like, was day to day!
Whene'er I looked, thy Image still was there;
It trembled, but it never passed away.

How perfect was the calm! it seemed no sleep;
No mood, which season takes away, or brings:
I could have fancied that the mighty Deep
Was even the gentlest of all gentle Things.

Ah! then, if mine had been the Painter's hand,
To express what then I saw; and add the gleam,
The light that never was, on sea or land,
The consecration, and the Poet's dream;

I would have planted thee, thou hoary Pile
Amid a world how different from this!
Beside a sea that could not cease to smile;
On tranquil land, beneath a sky of bliss...

A Picture had it been of lasting ease,
Elysian quiet, without toil or strife;
No motion but the moving tide, a breeze,
Or merely silent Nature's breathing life.

Such, in the fond illusion of my heart,
Such Picture would I at the time have made:
And seen the soul of truth in every part,
A steadfast peace that might not be betrayed.

So once it would have been, – 'tis so no more;
I have submitted to a new control:
A power is gone, which nothing can restore;
A deep distress hath humanised my Soul.

Then, Beaumont, Friend! who would have been
                             the Friend,
If he had lived, of Him whom I deplore,
This work of thine I blame not, but commend;
This sea in anger, and that dismal shore.

O 'tis a passionate Work! yet wise and well,
Well chosen is the spirit that is here;
That Hulk which labours in the deadly swell,
This rueful sky, this pageantry of fear!

And this huge Castle, standing here sublime,
I love to see the look with which it braves,
Cased in the unfeeling armour of old time,
The lightning, the fierce wind, and trampling waves.

Farewell, farewell the heart that lives alone,
Housed in a dream, at distance from the Kind!
Such happiness, wherever it be known,
Is to be pitied; for 'tis surely blind.

But welcome fortitude, and patient cheer,
And frequent sights of what is to be borne!
Such sights, or worse, as are before me here, –
Not without hope we suffer and we moan.

William Wordsworth
1770-1850

Calm after Hurricane at Patterdale

The storm is past; the raging wind no more,
Between the mountains rushing, sweeps the vale,
Washing the billows of the troubled lake
High into the air; the snowy fleece lies thick;
From every bough, from every jutting rock
The crystals hang; the torrent's roar has ceased –
As if that Voice that called Creation forth
Had said 'Be Still.'   All nature stands aghast
Suspended by the viewless power of cold.

Elizabeth Smith
1776-1803

I Wandered Lonely as a Cloud

I wandered lonely as a cloud
  That floats on high o'er vales and hills,
When all at once I saw a crowd,
  A host, of golden daffodils;
Beside the lake, beneath the trees,
Fluttering and dancing in the breeze.

Continuous as the stars that shine
  And twinkle on the milky way,
They stretched in never-ending line
  Along the margin of a bay:
Ten thousand saw I at a glance,
Tossing their heads in sprightly dance.

The waves beside them danced; but they
  Out-did the sparkling waves in glee:
A poet could not but be gay,
  In such a jocund company:
I gazed – and gazed – but little thought
What wealth the show to me had bought:

For oft, when on my couch I lie
  In vacant or in pensive mood,
They flash upon that inward eye
  Which is the bliss of solitude;
And then my heart with pleasure fills,
And dances with the daffodils.

William Wordsworth
1770-1850

If Thoughts Were Flowers

If thoughts were flowers, and words could heal our pain,
I would give my friend a garden filled with songbirds
Where tree leaves whisper to a stream
And summer evenings hang with the scent of warm gold sun
The petals floating for her bed, soft as heather wine.

And on the tops of the hills, around where the garden lies,
I would gather wood in piles and set a ring of fires
To destroy the frosts of winter and singe the storm clouds
With their dragon tongues.

And if flowers were thoughts, the blue of the gentian
Would humble my words for ever and, in the cathedral of trees,
Peace would descend like pollen motes upon our hair.

David Lyons

Lines from 'The Prelude'

Within the Vale
Of Nightshade, to St. Mary's honour built,
Stands yet a mouldering pile with fractured arch,
Belfry, and images, and living trees;
A holy scene! – Along the smooth green turf
Our horses grazed. To more than inland peace,
Left by the west wind sweeping overhead
From a tumultuous ocean, trees and towers
In that sequestered valley may be seen,
Both silent and both motionless alike;
Such the deep shelter that is there, and such
The safeguard for repose and quietness.

Our steeds remounted and the summons given,
With whip and spur we through the chauntry flew
In uncouth race, and left the cross-legged knight,
And the stone-abbot, and that single wren
Which one day sang so sweetly in the nave
Of the old church, that – though from recent showers
The earth was comfortless, and , touched by faint
Internal breezes, sobbings of the place
And respirations, from the roofless walls
The shuddering ivy dripped large drops – yet still
So sweetly 'mid the gloom the invisible bird
Sang to herself, that there I could have made
My dwelling-place, and lived for ever there
To hear such music.

William Wordsworth
1770-1850

Unexpected Beauty

It is only by the habit of representing faithfully all things, that we can truly learn what is beautiful, and what is not. The ugliest objects contain some elements of beauty; and in all it is an element peculiar to themselves, which cannot be separated from their ugliness, but must either be enjoyed together with it or not at all. The more a painter accepts nature as he finds it, the more unexpected beauty he discovers in what he at first despised; but once let him arrogate the right of rejection, and he will gradually contract his circle of enjoyment, until what he supposed to be nobleness of selection ends in narrowness of perception. Dwelling perpetually upon one class of ideas, his art becomes at once monstrous and morbid; until at last he cannot faithfully represent even what he chooses to retain; his discrimination contracts into darkness, and his fastidiousness fades into fatuity.

John Ruskin
1819-1900

From 'The Prelude'

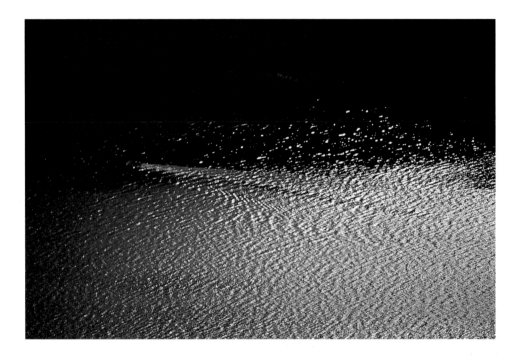

One summer evening (led by her) I found
A little boat tied to a willow tree
Within a rocky cave, its usual home.
Straight I unloosed her chain, and stepping in
Pushed from the shore. It was an act of stealth
And troubled pleasure, nor without the voice
Of mountain-echoes did my boat move on;
Leaving behind her still, on either side,
Small circles glittering idly in the moon,
Until they melted all into one track
Of sparkling light. But now, like one who rows,
Proud of his skill, to reach a chosen point
With an unswerving line, I fixed my view
Upon the summit of a craggy ridge,
The horizon's utmost boundary; far above
Was nothing but the stars and the grey sky.
She was an elfin pinnacle; lustily
I dipped my oars into the silent lake,
And, as I rose upon the stroke,my boat
Went heaving through the water like a swan;
When, from behind that craggy steep till then
The horizon's bound, a huge peak, black and huge,
As if with voluntary power instinct,
Upreared its head. I struck and struck again,
And growing still in stature the grim shape
Towered up between me and the stars, and still,
For so it seemed, with purpose of its own
And measured motion like a living thing,

Strode after me. With trembling oars I turned,
And through the silent water stole my way
Back to the covert of the willow tree;
There in her mooring-place I left my bark, –
And through the meadows homeward went, in grave
And serious mood; but after I had seen
That spectacle, for many days my brain
Worked with a dim and undetermined sense
Of unknown modes of being; o'er my thoughts
There hung a darkness, call it solitude
Or blank desertion. No familiar shapes
Remained, no pleasant images of trees,
Of sea or sky, no colours of green fields;
But huge and mighty forms, that do not live
Like living men, moved slowly through the mind
By day, and were a trouble to my dreams.

William Wordsworth
1770-1850

61

This is the Spot

This is the spot: – how mildly does the sun
Shine in between the fading leaves! the air
In the habitual silence of this wood
Is more than silent; and this bed of heath –
Where shall we find so sweet a resting-place?
Come, let me see thee sink into a dream
Of quiet thoughts, protracted till thine eye
Be calm as water when the winds are gone
And no one can tell whither. My sweet Friend,
We two have had such happy hours together
That my heart melts in me to think of it.

William Wordsworth
1770-1850

Long Meg and her Daughters

A weight of awe, not easy to be borne,
Fell suddenly upon my Spirit – cast
From the dread bosom of the unknown past,
When first I saw that family forlorn.
Speak Thou, whose massy strength and stature scorn
The power of years – pre-eminent, and placed
Apart, to overlook the circle vast –
Speak, Giant-mother! tell it to the Morn
While she dispels the cumbrous shades of Night;
Let the Moon hear, emerging from a cloud;
At whose behest uprose on British ground
That Sisterhood, in hieroglyphic round
Forth-shadowing, some have deemed, the infinite
The inviolable God, that tames the proud!

William Wordsworth
1770-1850